Original title:
The Joy Inside

Copyright © 2024 Creative Arts Management OÜ
All rights reserved.

Author: Sophia Kingsley
ISBN HARDBACK: 978-9916-88-884-1
ISBN PAPERBACK: 978-9916-88-885-8

Sparks of Liveliness in Stillness

In the hush of dawn's embrace,
A flicker dances in the light,
Each breath a spark, a gentle trace,
Nature wakes, bids dreams take flight.

Whispers glide on morning air,
Moments pause, yet hearts will race,
In the stillness, joys laid bare,
Life ignites in every space.

The Secret Garden of Merriment

Behind the gate where laughter blooms,
Colors spill on verdant ground,
Each petal hums, dispels the glooms,
In every corner, joy is found.

Sunshine dances on leaves anew,
Children's giggles weave through trees,
In this realm where dreams come true,
The essence of pure happiness breathes.

Threads of Warmth in Cold Days

When the chill bites, and shadows creep,
Gather close, let spirits soar,
In the hearth's glow, memories seep,
Woven warmth, a cozy store.

Hands entwined, hearts pulsing strong,
Stories shared in the flicker's gleam,
In winter's grasp, we still belong,
Threads of love, a timeless dream.

A Symphony of Quiet Ecstasy

In the silence, melodies rise,
Notes like whispers in the night,
Stars above, a canvas of skies,
Each heartbeat swells, pure delight.

Moonlight bathes the world in peace,
Every shadow softly sways,
In this pause, our worries cease,
Finding bliss in tranquil ways.

Compositions of Cheerful Remembrance

In bright halls of laughter we sing,
Memories dance on the whispering breeze.
Each moment a note, a joy to bring,
Together we cherish, hearts at ease.

The sun paints our faces with gold,
As stories of old weave a tender thread.
With every smile, new tales unfold,
In the album of life, where love is spread.

Trails of Gratefulness

On pathways paved with gratitude's glow,
Each step a reminder of blessings dear.
Nature's embrace, in its gentle flow,
Whispers of thanks are all we hear.

With every sunrise, hope is renewed,
Raindrops like jewels on leaves do cling.
In silence we find, our hearts imbued,
With joy that the simple moments bring.

The Secret Well of Serenity

Beneath the tumult, a haven lies,
A tranquil pool, where troubles cease.
In the depths, reflection softly sighs,
Pulling the heart towards quiet peace.

Here whispers of calm in shadows dwell,
With every breath, the worries unfurl.
In this hidden cave, we weave our spell,
A gentle embrace in a chaotic world.

Flickers of Delight

In twilight's glow, a spark ignites,
Dance of fireflies in evening's sway.
Each twinkle a promise that ignites,
Fleeting moments that brighten the gray.

Through laughter and joy, our spirits soar,
Like petals afloat on a warm summer's night.
These flickers of joy, we always adore,
In the tapestry of life, they shine so bright.

Sublime Moments

In twilight's gentle grace we stand,
The whispers of the night so grand.
Stars awaken, soft and bright,
Guiding us through the tranquil night.

Each heartbeat echoes with delight,
Embracing dreams that take to flight.
Moments cherished, pure and true,
In the stillness, me and you.

The Essence of Uplift

A breeze ignites the calm within,
Where worries fade and hopes begin.
With every step on path anew,
Life unfolds, revealing view.

Soft laughter dances in the air,
Moments shared beyond compare.
In every smile, a spark ignites,
Lifting hearts to wondrous heights.

Embrace of Warmth

In cozy corners hearts entwine,
With tender words, our souls align.
A gentle touch, a loving gaze,
Filling moments with a warm blaze.

As sunlight streams through window panes,
Comfort flows like gentle rains.
Together wrapped in love's embrace,
We find our healing, find our space.

Unfolding the Inner Glow

Within us lies a radiant spark,
A glimmer found within the dark.
With every breath, we come alive,
Embracing all that helps us thrive.

Let passions surge and worries fade,
In this journey, never weighed.
With strength and grace, we gently rise,
Unfolding dreams beneath the skies.

Gentle Waves of Fulfillment

Softly lap the shores of dreams,
Whispers of hope carried on streams.
Every tide brings a story anew,
Embracing paths we long to pursue.

In the stillness of twilight's glow,
Promises made in the ebb and flow.
Hearts aglow with a radiant grace,
Finding peace in this sacred space.

Like grains of sand, we weave and blend,
In unity, our spirits ascend.
With each wave, we rise and fall,
In the dance of life, we hear the call.

Together we sail, side by side,
On the gentle current, we abide.
Hand in hand, we touch the sky,
In these waves, we learn to fly.

The Canvas of Inner Peace

Brush of stillness sweeps the night,
Colors blend in soft moonlight.
Every stroke a moment's grace,
Awakening the heart's embrace.

Whispers of silence paint the air,
Notes of calm replace despair.
With each hue, a dream appears,
Washing away the lingering fears.

In the quiet, visions grow,
Framing life in a tranquil flow.
Every shade a whispered prayer,
Wrapping the soul in gentle care.

Thus we find the art of being,
In the end, it's love we're seeing.
Canvas stretched, the colors blend,
Peaceful heart, our constant friend.

Dancing with the Stars Above

In the velvet sky, we twirl and sway,
Guided by stars that light the way.
Each spark a promise, bright and bold,
Whispers of stories waiting to be told.

With every spin, we chase our dreams,
Under the moon's soft silver beams.
Celestial melodies fill the night,
We dance in joy, hearts taking flight.

Hands extended to worlds unseen,
In the cosmic ballet, we glean.
Footprints in stardust, forever ours,
Lost in the grace of celestial stars.

Together we glide through endless skies,
In the light, our spirit flies.
Boundless love in the night we claim,
In the dance of life, we find our name.

Beneath the Veil of Ordinary Days

In the morning light, shadows play,
Simple joys fill the heart each day.
Moments quiet, yet deeply felt,
Beneath the surface, secrets melt.

The laughter shared, the stories told,
In every glance, life's beauty unfolds.
Tenderness hides in mundane things,
In the routine, a soft heart sings.

Brick by brick, we build our dreams,
Sipping tea by sunlit streams.
Finding magic in the small and plain,
In every drop, love's sweet refrain.

So cherish the days wrapped in disguise,
For in the ordinary, eternity lies.
Through fleeting hours, treasure remains,
Beneath the veil, life's love sustains.

Inner Sunshine

In shadows deep, a glow does rise,
A spark ignites within the skies.
With every breath, a light we find,
A gentle warmth that soothes the mind.

Through storms that shake, we stand so tall,
Embrace the light, let darkness fall.
In every heart, a sunbeam shines,
Together bright, our love defines.

We gather strength, together whole,
With open hearts, we share our soul.
In laughter's grace, our spirits soar,
A dance of joy, forevermore.

A Collection of Gleeful Moments

A whisper soft, the breeze does sing,
In every heart, the joy takes wing.
A moment shared, a smile so bright,
The world transformed by pure delight.

Skip through the fields, let worries fade,
In gentle rays, our fears are laid.
A treasured laugh, a memory made,
In simple joys, our dreams cascade.

The sun above, a golden hue,
In every glance, we find what's true.
With friends beside, we chase the day,
In gleeful moments, come what may.

Hues of Happiness

In every color, joy is found,
A spectrum bright, where dreams abound.
With every shade, a story told,
In painted skies, our hearts unfold.

The blush of dawn, the twilight's gleam,
In hues of hope, we craft our dream.
A splash of laughter, a touch of grace,
Together we light this blessed space.

In vibrant tones, our spirits rise,
With every brush, the beauty lies.
In unity, we paint our skies,
With hues of happiness, love never dies.

Resilient Radiance

In shadows deep, the light will gleam,
A heart of steel, yet soft as cream.
Through storms we grow, we rise anew,
With every step, we find our view.

The fire within, it burns so bright,
A guiding star in darkest night.
With courage strong, we face our fears,
And through the trials, shed our tears.

Rooted in Serenity

In quiet earth, the roots entwine,
A tranquil space, where hearts align.
With gentle winds, we sway and bend,
As peace and love become our trend.

The whispering trees, they tell our tales,
Of calm and hope as the heart sails.
In harmony, we find our way,
With every breath, a brand new day.

Cradled in Goodness

In tender arms, we find our place,
Where kindness blooms, and hearts embrace.
With every smile, the world ignites,
A gentle spark that fills the nights.

Through simple acts of love we share,
Compassion binds us, ever rare.
In every heart, a story grows,
Of all the beauty that life knows.

Streams of Smiles

In rivers bright, the laughter flows,
A vibrant dance where happiness grows.
With every wave, a joy released,
The heart finds comfort, love increased.

As sunbeams play on cheerful streams,
We chase our hopes, fulfill our dreams.
In every glance, a world is found,
Where smiles abound, and love is crowned.

Uplifted Hearts

In the morning light, we rise anew,
With dreams in our eyes and skies of blue.
Together we stand, hand in hand,
Our spirits soar high, like a band.

Through laughter and tears, we find our way,
With love as our guide, we'll never sway.
The warmth of our hearts, a golden spark,
Illuminates the path, lighting the dark.

Each step we take, a journey profound,
In the rhythm of life, our joys unbound.
We dance in the rain, we sing in the sun,
With uplifted hearts, we've only begun.

The Secret Garden of Happiness

In a garden unseen, where the wildflowers grow,
Whispers of joy in the soft breezes blow.
With petals like laughter, in colors so bright,
We nurture our souls in the warm sunlight.

The brook hums a tune, a melody sweet,
As we wander through dreams, where hearts gently meet.
Here in the silence, our secrets we share,
In the hush of the moment, we banish despair.

With each blossomed thought, our spirits take flight,
In this secret abode, we bask in delight.
The fragrance of love, forever will stay,
In the garden of happiness, we'll play every day.

Sparkles of Contentment

In the still of the night, stars twinkle bright,
Each spark is a wish, a shimmering light.
Contentment unfolds like a cozy embrace,
In the heart's quiet moments, we find our place.

With laughter that dances on gentle winds,
The beauty of life, where true joy begins.
In the hum of the world, we pause and we sigh,
Finding peace in the now, as time drifts by.

Each day we gather these bright little beams,
Floating like bubbles in our sweetest dreams.
Sparkles of joy, in our lives, we ignite,
Creating a tapestry of pure delight.

Echoes of Bliss

In the stillness of dawn, whispers unfold,
Echoes of bliss, in the stories retold.
With hearts that are open, we sail through the day,
Finding beauty in moments that rarely delay.

The laughter of friends, a harmonious song,
In the rhythm of life, where we all belong.
Through shadows and light, our spirits entwine,
In the echoes of bliss, our love will shine.

Each smile a reminder, each hug a warm glow,
In the tapestry woven, our happiness flows.
With gratitude held, we cherish the past,
In the echoes of bliss, true joy is steadfast.

Melodies of Unseen Elation

In the quiet dusk, whispers play,
A gentle tune, guiding my way.
Stars awaken in the twilight sky,
Under their gaze, my spirit can fly.

Laughter lingers in the soft air,
Notes of joy danced without a care.
Heartbeat echoes in rhythmic grace,
Finding the magic in time and space.

With every breeze, a sweet refrain,
Moments wrapped in a tender chain.
Unseen elation fills the night,
In these melodies, my soul takes flight.

Here where the shadows softly blend,
Each note a promise, a silent friend.
Melodies weave through heart and mind,
A harmony of the rarest kind.

The Smile that Lives Within

In the mirror's gaze, a secret holds,
A gentle spark that never grows old.
With every breath, it softly shines,
Reflecting joy in mysterious lines.

Through trials faced and shadows cast,
This inner light will ever last.
A quiet courage roots itself deep,
In the heart's chambers, a treasure to keep.

When the world feels heavy and torn,
The smile within helps souls reborn.
With every heartbeat, it starts anew,
Dancing brightly in shades of blue.

In silent moments, it can be found,
A gentle whisper, a soothing sound.
The smile that lives, both fierce and kind,
A testament to the love we find.

Unfurling Petals of Contentment

In the dawning light, flowers bloom,
Petals unfurl, dispelling gloom.
With colors bright, they greet the morn,
In their embrace, new joys are born.

Each layer opens, revealing grace,
Nature's whispers in a sacred space.
Contentment flows through every thread,
In the garden of dreams, hope is spread.

Butterflies dance with gentle ease,
A ballet performed by the summer breeze.
In this stillness, life finds its way,
Unfurling petals greet the day.

With every fragrance, a story told,
Moments cherished, memories bold.
This beauty, rich in simple delight,
Unfurls within, a canvas of light.

A Tapestry of Inner Sunshine

Crafted threads of golden hue,
Woven tales that feel so true.
Every stitch a vibrant chord,
In the heart, a joyful hoard.

Through stormy days and skies so gray,
Inner sunshine lights the way.
In quiet corners, it softly gleams,
Binding together our fondest dreams.

Colors blend in a warm embrace,
Creating harmony in this space.
A tapestry of moments divine,
Worn with pride, this heart of mine.

As days unfold, the patterns shift,
Each new thread a precious gift.
In every heart, a spark remains,
A tapestry where love sustains.

Cascades of Laughter

Laughter spills like water, soft
Rolling down the hills of joy,
In every echo, smiles are caught,
A moment's bliss, a heart's envoy.

Children dance beneath the trees,
Giggling as the sunshine beams,
Their bubbling joy, a gentle breeze,
In merry tunes, we find our dreams.

With every chuckle, worries fade,
The world transforms in golden hue,
A symphony of joy is played,
In cascading laughter, hearts renew.

Together we create a song,
A melody of bright delight,
In laughter's arms, we all belong,
As day drifts softly into night.

Boundless Gleam

Stars twinkle in the velvet sky,
Each a wish, a silent spark,
They guide our hearts, as time slips by,
A luminescent, radiant arc.

In gentle waves, the moonlight spreads,
Kissing the earth with silver grace,
In whispered dreams, our spirit treads,
Embracing hope in every place.

The night unfolds its glittering cloak,
As shadows dance, we breathe in deep,
In every moment, love awoke,
In boundless gleam, our secrets keep.

Together we forge paths of light,
Through darkness, we will always roam,
With hearts ablaze, we'll soar in flight,
In boundless gleam, we find our home.

Heart's Echoes of Contentment

In a cozy nook, we sit tonight,
With whispers soft like twilight's glow,
Contentment blooms in sweet delight,
As gentle breezes come and go.

Every smile, a cherished line,
In the book of life, we share our tales,
Together we find a love divine,
As soft as whispers in the gales.

With hands entwined, no need for words,
Our hearts converse in silent beats,
In peace, we find the world prefers,
The echoing rhythm of love's retreats.

Beneath the stars, our wishes blend,
Each heartbeat draws us close, anew,
In this calm space, we are more than friends,
Our hearts' echoes hold love's true hue.

Celestial Murmurs of Cheer

In quiet nights, as dreams take flight,
The stars conspire with glimmers bright,
Each whispering breeze, a soft embrace,
Celestial murmurs fill the space.

With every dawn, the sun awakes,
Warming the world with gentle grace,
Its rays bring hope, as shadows flee,
Turning whispers into harmony.

We laugh and play beneath the skies,
With hearts like kites, we rise and soar,
In every moment, joy complies,
In celestial cheer, we seek for more.

Together we spin tales of old,
In light and warmth, our spirits cheer,
In every heartbeat, love unfolds,
With celestial murmurs, we draw near.

Heartstrings Pulled by Delight

In the whisper of dawn's soft glow,
Laughter dances where memories flow.
Each moment a treasure, pure and sweet,
A melody played on a heart's heartbeat.

Sunshine paints shadows bright and bold,
Stories of warmth in the winter's cold.
Every smile a blink of the soul's delight,
Pulling heartstrings, setting spirits in flight.

With every fleeting glance we share,
The world blossoms in colors rare.
Tugging gently on the threads of hope,
We find our way, together we cope.

In the embrace of joy, we stand,
Hand in hand, a promise so grand.
For in each heartbeat lies a chance,
To dance through life in a sweet romance.

Embracing the Colors of Euphoria

With every brushstroke of the morn,
Painted skies where dreams are born.
Radiant hues that kiss the air,
Whispers of joy, a vibrant prayer.

In fields of gold, beneath the sun,
Laughter bubbles, hearts become one.
Each petal sings a song of cheer,
Inviting us closer, drawing near.

Dancing through rainbows, we explore,
Every shade a promise of more.
Euphoria blooms in laughter's embrace,
Celebrating life in this sacred space.

As twilight drapes its gentle shroud,
We stand together, lost in the crowd.
Colorful moments etched in our hearts,
Waiting for dawn, where love never departs.

The Dance of Serendipity

In the realm where fate intertwines,
Moments like stars—serendipitous signs.
Paths cross gently, fate takes a spin,
Where unexpected joys quietly begin.

A chance encounter, a spark in the night,
Echoes of laughter, pure delight.
Whispers of fortune linger in the air,
Guiding us softly, leading us there.

The dance of the heart, a rhythm so true,
Life gets a glow through a friend like you.
Every twirl brings a twist, a turn,
In the dance of life, so much to learn.

With each step, we embrace the thrill,
The magic of moments that time cannot still.
Hand in hand, we'll journey along,
Writing our story to an eternal song.

Moments of Pure Wonder

In stillness found on a starlit night,
The world unveils its dazzling sight.
A hush of magic fills the air,
Moments so rare, beyond compare.

With every heartbeat, a truth unfolds,
Secrets of life in whispers told.
Nature's canvas, awe-inspiring grace,
Inviting us closer to discover our place.

With eyes wide open, we soak it all in,
The warmth of the sun, the gentle wind.
Each second a gift, a treasure to find,
Moments of wonder forever enshrined.

In the dance of the cosmos, we sway,
Finding joy in the small things each day.
A tapestry woven, forever profound,
In moments of wonder, our hearts are unbound.

Heartbeats of Unspoken Happiness

In whispers soft, the joy resides,
A dance of light, where love abides.
Each quiet smile, a bond so tight,
In shadows deep, we find our light.

A secret shared, in silence sweet,
Heartbeats echo, a gentle beat.
In every glance, a story told,
Of hearts entwined, in warmth and gold.

Beneath the stars, where dreams take flight,
In silent hopes, we chase the night.
The world may fade, but we stand true,
In every heart, a hope anew.

Untamed Laughter of the Soul

A chuckle breaks, the air it fills,
In joyful moments, time stands still.
With wild abandon, spirits soar,
In laughter's grace, we want no more.

Each giggle dances, light takes flight,
In playful jests, we find our light.
The echoes ring, through valleys wide,
In every heart, our joy can hide.

A symphony of glee unfurled,
In every child, the laughter swirled.
With simple joys, we find our way,
In untamed laughs, we seize the day.

Echoes of Serenity in a Chaotic World

Amid the storm, a whisper calls,
In every heart, where peace befalls.
Through frantic days, we seek to find,
The quiet grace that soothes the mind.

In gentle breezes, calm arrives,
A tranquil heart, where stillness thrives.
Through chaos fierce, we stand our ground,
In whispered prayers, our strength is found.

The world may spin, in frantic pace,
Yet in our hearts, we find our space.
With every breath, we ground our souls,
In echoes soft, tranquility rolls.

The Radiance Within the Everyday

In morning light, a world unfolds,
Each simple moment, a treasure holds.
With every glance, the magic lies,
In fleeting hours, time softly flies.

The laughter shared, the hands that meet,
In tiny gestures, life feels sweet.
The fragrance of flowers, the warmth of sun,
In daily rhythms, we become one.

A cup of tea, a book's embrace,
In mundane joys, we find our place.
With eyes wide open, we start to see,
The radiance shines, in you and me.

Colors of Inner Bliss

In the garden of my mind, so bright,
Blossoms bloom in pure delight.
Shades of laughter, hues of grace,
Each moment's glow, a warm embrace.

Waves of joy flow like a stream,
Whispers soft as nature's dream.
Crimson, azure, emerald light,
Painting shadows, banishing night.

Gentle breezes carry peace,
In this realm, my soul's release.
Brushstrokes vivid, wild and free,
Colors dance in harmony.

Every hue a heart's refrain,
In this bliss, I'm whole again.
A masterpiece that brings me near,
To the love that conquers fear.

Ethereal Flavors of Happiness

Sweet nectar drips from golden skies,
Tasting joy through laughter's cries.
Sunlight warms the spirit's zest,
In this feast, my heart finds rest.

Like a breeze with hints of spice,
Each moment savored, oh so nice.
Honeyed whispers fill the air,
With every thought, I'm light as air.

Fruits of kindness, ripe with care,
Banquets shared, beyond compare.
Savoring smiles, we celebrate,
In this realm, love's on our plate.

Ethereal flavors, pure delight,
Dancing souls embrace the light.
Every taste, a memory we keep,
In the heart's pantry, love runs deep.

Anthem of the Heart

Beat by beat, the rhythm grows,
In every pulse, true love bestows.
Melodies rise, soft and clear,
An anthem sung for all to hear.

Chords of friendship, woven tight,
Harmonies that spark the night.
Voices join in sweet refrain,
Together, we embrace the plain.

Notes cascading like a stream,
Dreams alive in vibrant theme.
Every heart a sacred song,
Together, we forever belong.

In this symphony of light,
Love's embrace turns dark to bright.
An anthem echoing through time,
With every beat, our spirits climb.

Shining Threads of Positivity

Weaving light from moments small,
Threads of gold, we share with all.
In every smile, a spark ignites,
Together, we illuminate the nights.

Patterns bright through trials pave,
Hand in hand, we will be brave.
Every challenge, just a part,
Of intricate designs of heart.

Woven tightly, dreams take flight,
In this tapestry of light.
Each stitch a story, bold and true,
In unity, we start anew.

Shining threads that bind us near,
Filling lives with hope and cheer.
In every color, every line,
Positivity's glow, forever shine.

Enchanted Heartbeats

In twilight's glow, soft whispers play,
A dance of shadows, where dreams sway.
With every pulse, the stars align,
In enchanted moments, hearts entwine.

Beneath the moon, where secrets hide,
A symphony of love, in silence, bide.
Each heartbeat echoes, a story told,
In tender embraces, warmth unfolds.

The nightingale sings of love's sweet grace,
In every note, a familiar face.
Together we soar on wings of light,
In this enchanted realm, all feels right.

With every breath, the magic grows,
In the garden of dreams, where passion flows.
A tapestry woven, both wild and free,
In the pulse of the night, just you and me.

Mosaic of Tranquil Joys

Colors of life in vibrant hues,
A canvas painted with laughter's muse.
Each moment stitched with threads of gold,
In this mosaic, our stories unfold.

Breezes carry the scent of grace,
In every smile, a warm embrace.
From whispered hopes to dreams that soar,
In tranquil joys, we seek for more.

A symphony hums in the gentle breeze,
Nature's soft lullaby, putting hearts at ease.
Each petal and leaf sings harmony,
In this mosaic, we find unity.

With open arms, together we stand,
Creating a world, so soft and grand.
In vibrant echoes, let spirits play,
In joyful moments, forever stay.

Trails of Lightheartedness

Footsteps tracing in the warm sunlight,
Dancing through shadows, a pure delight.
In laughter's echo, the world is bright,
On trails of light, everything feels right.

The trees sway gently, a playful song,
Inviting us to join, where we belong.
With every step, the worries fade,
In lighthearted leaps, our dreams are made.

Clouds drift lazily across the sky,
As our spirits lift, we learn to fly.
With hearts unburdened, we chase the day,
On trails of joy, we find our way.

In the dance of time, we hold the key,
To cherish the moments, wild and free.
In simple pleasures, love's embrace,
With every heartbeat, we find our place.

Breaths of Inner Peace

In stillness found, a gentle sigh,
Where worries fade and spirits fly.
A quiet moment, soft and slow,
In breaths of peace, our essence grows.

The world outside may rush and race,
But here within, we find our space.
With every inhale, calm descends,
In sacred pauses, the heart mends.

Whispers of nature call us near,
In tranquil waves, we shed our fear.
With open hearts, we greet the day,
In breaths of peace, we find our way.

Together we journey, hand in hand,
In this serene and sacred land.
As we navigate life's gentle stream,
In breaths of peace, we live the dream.

Fabrics of Exuberance

Woven threads of joy abound,
Colorful patterns all around.
Each stitch a moment, bright and bold,
In every heart, a story told.

Laughter dances through the loom,
Spinning light dispels the gloom.
Textures soft, with warmth we share,
In the fabric, love laid bare.

Joyful colors blend and weave,
Echoes of what we believe.
In every tug, a vivid dream,
A tapestry of pure esteem.

With hands united, we create,
Exuberance, we celebrate.
In this fabric, lives entwine,
A masterpiece, divine design.

Soft Radiations of Happiness

Gentle beams from morning's light,
Embrace us with warmth so bright.
A smile dances on each face,
In happiness, we find our place.

Sunbeams flicker, shadows play,
Softly guiding us each day.
Echoes of laughter fill the air,
In every moment, sweetness there.

Whispers of joy in sunlit rays,
Bathe our souls in golden praise.
Tender hearts, in blissful sway,
Cherish love, come what may.

With every hug, each heartfelt cheer,
Radiations that draw us near.
In harmony, we find our tune,
Soft radiations, hearts in bloom.

A Journey into Light

Step by step, the path unfolds,
Guided by the light it holds.
With every footfall, dreams ignite,
In every shadow, gleams so bright.

Beyond the dusk, the dawn will rise,
In gentle hues, the day complies.
A journey filled with hope and grace,
In every moment, we embrace.

Stars guide us through the night,
Illuminating truths with might.
Together we will pave the way,
Into the dawn of each new day.

With hearts aglow, we roam the land,
Side by side, forever hand in hand.
A luminous path, our spirits soar,
A journey into light, forevermore.

Murmurs of Pure Enjoyment

In whispers soft, the moments creep,
A sigh of joy, in silence deep.
Every heartbeat sings a tune,
Murmurs of joy, beneath the moon.

Laughter echoes in the air,
Simple pleasures, we all share.
Amidst the chaos, peace we find,
In every petal, love entwined.

Tales of delight stir in the breeze,
Bring forth a warmth that aims to please.
Gentle waves of pure delight,
Wrap our spirits, hold them tight.

In every smile, in every glance,
Life invites us to this dance.
Murmurs of enjoyment fill the night,
In every heart, a beacon bright.

The Light Beneath the Surface

In the depths where silence lies,
A shimmer breaks, a sweet surprise.
Waves of whispers softly glow,
A world unseen begins to flow.

Beneath the calm, the spirits dance,
In hidden realms, they take their chance.
A twinkle shines, a fleeting sight,
Illuminating the quiet night.

Secrets stir on gentle streams,
Fading in and out of dreams.
With every pulse, the light expands,
Carrying hope in guiding hands.

Awakening the shades of grey,
Transforming night to brightening day.
For in the dark, the truth can gleam,
Revealing all that once did dream.

Serene Ripples of Gratitude

In tranquil pools, reflections blend,
Whispers of thanks that never end.
Every ripple, a gentle sigh,
Carried on, as moments fly.

Softly stirring, the heart expands,
In gratitude, the spirit stands.
A melody of love takes flight,
Extending grace, igniting light.

The sun dips low, its warmth embraced,
With open arms, the world is graced.
Each pause nurtures the soul's delight,
In stillness found, in soft twilight.

In every breath, a chance to feel,
The simple joys, the kind and real.
Serene ripples, a vibrant hue,
A dance of love for me and you.

Blossoms of Inner Harmony

In gardens deep, where silence reigns,
Blossoms bloom, releasing pains.
Petals whisper in vibrant hues,
As nature's song begins to muse.

With every twist, a tale unfolds,
Of strength in roots and dreams retold.
Harmony hums through earthy sighs,
As colors blend beneath the skies.

From shadows rise, the fruits of peace,
In unity, the heart's release.
Fragrant moments fill the air,
Blossoms swaying, free from care.

Letting go, embracing the now,
A peaceful heart, a solemn vow.
In stillness find the dance of grace,
Blossoms bloom in sacred space.

Glimmers of Hope in the Shadows

In corners dark where doubts may creep,
Glimmers shine, the promises keep.
Flickers of light, a soft caress,
Whispers of faith in the wilderness.

Through tangled paths and veils of night,
Courage glows, igniting bright.
In heavy hearts, a spark ignites,
Chasing away the fleeting frights.

With every breath, a chance to rise,
To see the dawn beyond the lies.
Hope unfurls, a gentle kiss,
Transforming shadows into bliss.

Together we find, hand in hand,
The strength that blooms across the land.
For in the dark, the stars will gleam,
Guiding us forward, beyond the dream.

Unwritten Verses of Glee

In the dawn of dreams we stand,
Hopes like petals in a hand.
Laughter dances on the breeze,
Woven softly 'neath the trees.

Every heartbeat sings a song,
Echoing where we belong.
Joyful glimmers in the night,
Moments woven into light.

With each step, our spirits soar,
Seeking what we're meant for more.
Fields of wonder stretch ahead,
Where our souls are gently led.

Together we will write the lines,
In a world where love entwines.
Every whisper, soft and clear,
Marks the path of those we cheer.

Fragments of Pure Ecstasy

In the twilight, colors blend,
Dreams and whispers never end.
Stars align with thoughts so bright,
Guiding hearts through velvet night.

Each moment holds a spark anew,
Drawing forth the joys we knew.
Life, a tapestry of threads,
Filled with hope where love treads.

When souls touch, the world ignites,
Brightening even the darkest nights.
In the dance of shadows cast,
Fragments linger from the past.

With every pulse, we chase the fire,
Boundless joy, the heart's desire.
Lost in echoes of our song,
Fragments rise; we dance along.

Flutters of Delight

On gentle winds, our spirits fly,
Caressing dreams that fill the sky.
Mirthful whispers in the air,
Silver laughs, light as a prayer.

Petals fall like secrets shared,
In our hearts, the world is bared.
Every glimmer paints our soul,
In this moment, we feel whole.

Tickling thoughts like morning dew,
Embracing all the things we knew.
Joy unravels with each glance,
Leading us to sweet romance.

With every beat, delight's embrace,
Finding magic in each space.
Together in this wondrous plight,
We dance among the flutters bright.

A Canvas of Cherished Whispers

Upon a canvas, colors glint,
Every shade, a tender hint.
Stories weave in silken threads,
Carried softly where love leads.

In the hush, our hearts confide,
Moments where the dreams abide.
Brush of kindness, stroke of grace,
Painting smiles upon each face.

Every whisper brings alive,
Secrets where our spirits thrive.
In the gallery of our days,
Cherished echoes find their ways.

With each stroke, we leave our mark,
A masterpiece ignites the spark.
Together, in this artful dance,
We paint our world, a sweet romance.

Hidden Springs of Cheerfulness

In the heart of the meadow, laughter flows,
Among gentle petals, where the soft breeze goes.
Hidden springs of cheerfulness bubble with light,
Whispering secrets in the stillness of night.

Joy dances lightly on the tips of each blade,
Where shadows retreat and warm colors invade.
Each droplet of sunshine brings warmth to the soul,
Crafting moments of joy that make us feel whole.

In the laughter of children, echoing near,
In the rustling leaves, their whispers we hear.
Each hidden spring nurtures a garden so bright,
A place we can visit to rekindle delight.

Let's wander together where happiness lies,
In the hidden springs under vast, sunny skies.
Embrace all the wonders waiting for you,
In the heart of each moment, a joy ever true.

Whimsical Presences

In the twilight's glow, where shadows play,
Dancing sprites gather, welcoming the day.
With laughter that twinkles like stars in the night,
Whimsical presences bring pure delight.

They scatter the magic through every glen,
Tiptoeing softly o'er the backs of the wren.
With pockets of wonder and dreams to bestow,
They fill the night's canvas with vibrant glow.

Frolicsome creatures in fantastical hues,
Whispering secrets as the night bids adieu.
In the laughter of leaves and the moon's gentle light,
Whimsical presences make everything right.

Let's cherish the wonders that flutter and glide,
In the realm of enchantment, we'll joyfully ride.
With hearts wide open, let's dance through the night,
In the whimsical magic that fills us with light.

Tides of Elation

On shores of dreams where the waves kiss the sand,
Tides of elation swell and expand.
Each rhythm of laughter, buoyant and bright,
Carries whispers of joy on the soft moonlight.

The currents of gratitude flow like the sea,
As each high tide lifts spirits, setting them free.
A cascade of happiness washes ashore,
Opening hearts to all that we adore.

With each passing wave, a new chance to play,
Riding the swell of love's vibrant display.
In every crest, joy's radiant spark,
Illuminates pathways that lead from the dark.

So gather the moments like shells in a line,
Embrace the elation where hearts intertwine.
In the tides of life's ocean, let's dance and sway,
For together, we flourish, come what may.

Tapestry of Cheerful Dreams

Woven with threads of sunlight and glee,
A tapestry of dreams, vibrant and free.
Each color a memory, each stitch a laugh,
Crafting a portal to joy's gentle path.

In soft hues of dawn, where hopes take flight,
We sew kindred spirits, finding our light.
With whimsical patterns and visions that gleam,
We paint our existence in strokes of a dream.

The fabric of friendship warms every heart,
Stitched firmly together, never to part.
As we weave through the moments, hand in hand,
A masterpiece blooming across this vast land.

So let us create with love's gentle seam,
A tapestry woven with each cheerful dream.
With joy as our thread, let's expand and explore,
In the colors of life, forever we soar.

Glistening Perspectives

In the morning sun, we rise anew,
With every glance, the world is true.
Colors dance upon the dew,
A canvas bright, in every hue.

Through tangled paths, our spirits soar,
Finding beauty in each door.
Moments spark like never before,
Glistening tales in folklore.

A whisper of hope reaches out,
Chasing away the twitch of doubt.
Each heartbeat sings, a joyful shout,
In these perspectives, we no longer pout.

Embracing the Inner Light

Within our hearts, a flame does glow,
With every breath, let kindness flow.
Shadows vanish, courage to show,
Embrace the light, let your spirit grow.

The world outside can dim our view,
But deep inside, love sees us through.
In silent moments, dreams accrue,
Embracing all, for it is true.

A gentle touch can lift the night,
In shared laughter, we find our sight.
Together strong, our hope burns bright,
We hold each other, shining light.

A Tapestry of Cheer

In fields of green, joy intertwines,
With every smile, the heart aligns.
Threads of friendship, love defines,
A tapestry where laughter shines.

Each story woven, a moment shared,
With open arms, we show we cared.
From simple times, we are prepared,
In every smile, joy is declared.

A quilt of dreams, stitched tight with grace,
In every thread, a warm embrace.
Together strong, we find our place,
In this bright world, we set the pace.

The Unseen Happiness

Beneath the surface, joy resides,
In whispered winds and ocean tides.
A gentle pulse where hope abides,
The unseen happiness that guides.

In quiet moments, hearts align,
With every touch, a fragrant vine.
Hidden treasures we define,
In simple things, we find the sign.

The laughter shared, a fleeting glance,
In every breath, a second chance.
In the unspoken, we take a dance,
The unseen joys in life's expanse.

Veils of Cheer

In the morning light, they dance,
Joyful whispers on the breeze.
Laughter fills the vibrant space,
Each moment, hearts at ease.

Colors brush the waking sky,
A symphony of bright delight.
With every step, we rise and sway,
Together, chasing morning light.

Through fields of gold, we wander free,
Veils of cheer in every glance.
A tapestry of shared dreams,
Inviting all to join the dance.

In the evening's soft embrace,
We gather 'round the glowing fire.
Stories shared with warmth and grace,
Our spirits soar, reaching higher.

Shimmering Reflections

Beneath the moon, the waters gleam,
Stars scattered in the night.
Dreams float softly on the stream,
In shimmering, gentle light.

Ripples carry whispered tales,
Of travels far and wide.
Each reflection, secret veils,
In which the heart confides.

Waves of thought like brush strokes glide,
Painting stories on the shore.
In the stillness, truth abides,
Inviting us to seek for more.

In the depths, we find our way,
With courage, hope, and grace.
Shimmering dreams light our play,
In the night's warm embrace.

Embers of Blissful Thoughts

In the quiet, embers glow,
Carving warmth in twilight's hold.
Whispers soft, the breezes flow,
In moments tenderly told.

Thoughts like fireflies take their flight,
Dancing in the darkened air.
Each flicker brings a spark of light,
Enchanting hearts who dream and dare.

With every breath, a world unfolds,
Blissful echoes in the night.
Stories linger, sweet and bold,
Illuminating heart's delight.

Together, we chase thoughts that gleam,
In the warmth of friendship's glow.
Embers blend with every dream,
Through the night, our spirits flow.

Harmonies of Sweet Delight

In a garden where colors sing,
Nature whispers joy and peace.
Every petal, a tiny ring,
Creating moments that never cease.

Songs of birds in morning light,
Stirring hearts with soft refrain.
Every note, a pure delight,
Filling souls with joy again.

Dancing leaves in a gentle breeze,
Swaying to the rhythm divine.
Here, we find our hearts at ease,
In the beauty, we intertwine.

As twilight falls, the stars ignite,
A tapestry of wishes bright.
In this space, our dreams take flight,
Harmonies of sweet delight.

Whispers of Hidden Bliss

In twilight's embrace, softly they speak,
Hidden desires that linger and peek.
Gentle caress of the cool evening air,
Whispers of love, quiet and rare.

In gardens of dreams, where shadows play,
Secrets unfold in a magical way.
The heart's true rhythm, a melodious sigh,
Whispers of bliss, as the moments fly.

Stars weave their tales in a darkened sky,
A promise of joy that will never die.
In silence, we find the deepest of truths,
Whispers that guide our innocent youths.

With each whispered breath, an echo remains,
Binding our spirits, soft silken chains.
In hidden places, where souls intertwine,
Whispers of bliss, forever divine.

Radiant Echoes of Happiness

In laughter's embrace, bright echoes resound,
Dancing on air, love's rhythm is found.
Joy paints the canvas with vivid delight,
Radiant echoes that shimmer with light.

Every smile shared, a vibrant refrain,
Carved in our hearts, like a sweet refrain.
In moments so fleeting, but feelings so strong,
Echoes of happiness play our song.

With every heartbeat, we claim our bliss,
Woven together in moments like this.
The sun's gentle rays catch laughter's hue,
Radiant echoes, a love that's so true.

In shadows of doubt, let the light break through,
For happiness blossoms where love's in view.
With each step we take, let our spirits soar,
Radiant echoes, forever more.

Sunlit Secrets of the Heart

Beneath the bright sun, secrets reside,
In emerald meadows, our feelings can hide.
With petals of gold, like moments in time,
Sunlit secrets, in rhythm, they chime.

Gentle whispers of love, soft as the breeze,
Unravel the mysteries, put hearts at ease.
Upon the warm earth, where laughter is sown,
Sunlit secrets, in silence, are grown.

In the embrace of an afternoon glow,
The heart reveals what it longs to show.
Shadows retreat, where the passions ignite,
Sunlit secrets, blossoming bright.

With each tender glance, the world fades away,
A dance of two souls, where heartstrings convey.
In harmony's tune, our spirits shall part,
Sunlit secrets echo deep in the heart.

Laughter in the Silence

In quiet corners where shadows retreat,
Laughter finds solace, soft and discreet.
A spark in the dark, a glimmer of grace,
Laughter in silence, a warm embrace.

Moments of stillness, where hearts beat as one,
Whispers of joy in the absence of fun.
Echoes of giggles like ripples in time,
Laughter in the silence, a rhythm, a rhyme.

In the hush of the night, when the world is asleep,
Memories flourish, in laughter, we leap.
Bound by the joy that the night can unfold,
Laughter in silence, a treasure to hold.

With starlit connections, we treasure the sound,
In silence, we find what true love has found.
In shared silent moments, our spirits entwine,
Laughter in silence, a love so divine.

Celestial Dances of Tranquility

In twilight skies, the stars align,
A gentle sway, a cosmic sign.
Moonlight beams on tranquil seas,
Softly whispering with the breeze.

Galaxies spin in silent grace,
Each twirl a dream, a sacred place.
Comets trace their fleeting trails,
While time unveils what never fails.

Serenity wraps the world in light,
As planets waltz, a wondrous sight.
Harmony sings through endless night,
Where peace resides, pure and bright.

In this vast dome where echoes dwell,
Life's gentle rhythm casts a spell.
Dancing stars in a tranquil trance,
Invite the heart to take a chance.

The Uncharted Depths of Glee

In hidden caverns, joy does hide,
Where echoes play and thoughts collide.
Bubbles rise in laughter's tune,
Awakening dreams from slumber's ruin.

Surprises lurk in every nook,
Adventure calls from every book.
Each moment brims with glee unknown,
A treasure trove all on our own.

Through unmarked paths, we skip and sway,
With hearts ablaze, we find our way.
The world transforms with every leap,
In joy's embrace, our spirits creep.

As sunlight breaks on distant hills,
Laughter echoes, the heart fulfills.
In depths uncharted, we will be,
Boundless bliss, forever free.

Whispers of Elation

Softly spoken, sweet refrain,
In every heart, a joyful strain.
The morning sun, a tender kiss,
Brings forth the promise of pure bliss.

Gentle breezes carry dreams,
In lilac fields, the laughter gleams.
A symphony of nature's cheer,
Awakes the soul, dispels all fear.

Each fluttering leaf sings of grace,
As time slows down in this embrace.
In every smile, a spark ignites,
With whispers soft, the heart takes flight.

Through vibrant worlds where colors blend,
In elation's arms, our spirits mend.
Dancing shadows in the light,
Forever captured, pure delight.

Radiance Beneath the Surface

In quiet depths, a glow resides,
A hidden light that gently guides.
Beneath the waves, the secrets lay,
In sunlit realms that drift away.

Coral gardens, bright as day,
Hold stories of a vibrant play.
Colors flash and shadows twine,
Encasing beauty, so divine.

As currents weave their graceful dance,
Life flourishes in every chance.
Each heartbeat sings beneath the foam,
In this vast world, the heart finds home.

Emerging from the ocean's grace,
Radiance found in every space.
Let the depths unveil their truth,
For joy lies waiting, bold and smooth.

Sunrays Within

In the morning light we rise,
Golden beams that gently dance,
Whispers of the day's surprise,
A moment's shine, a fleeting chance.

Through the leaves, the sunlight streams,
Warming hearts that yearn to grow,
Sparking bright and tender dreams,
A gentle warmth, a soft glow.

Each ray holds a piece of grace,
Filling souls with radiant cheer,
In the stillness, we embrace,
The sunrays within, ever near.

Chasing Shadows of Laughter

In the twilight, shadows play,
Echoes of our joyful sound,
Chasing dreams that drift away,
In laughter's arms, we are found.

Underneath the fading light,
We run wild, both free and bold,
In the dance of day to night,
Glimmers of our stories told.

Each chuckle holds a spark,
Filling corners of the heart,
In the stillness, we embark,
On a journey, never part.

Blossoms of Bliss

In the garden, petals bloom,
Colors bright, a fragrant song,
In the air, dispelling gloom,
Where joys of life, forever throng.

With each blossom, whispers rise,
Nature's art, a sweet embrace,
Underneath the endless skies,
In every hue, we find our place.

Softly swaying in the breeze,
Time stands still; we breathe it in,
In this moment, hearts at ease,
Blossoms of bliss, where love begins.

Spheres of Innocent Wonder

In the quiet of the dawn,
Curiosity takes flight,
With each gaze, new worlds are drawn,
Innocence shines, pure and bright.

Round and round, the laughter swells,
In each bubble, dreams aglow,
Whispers of the stories tell,
Of the magic we all know.

Every twirl, a spark ignites,
A dance beneath the star-strewn skies,
In the heart, pure delight excites,
Spheres of wonder, where love lies.

Dance of the Heartstrings

In the glow of twilight's seam,
Hearts entwine, a whispered dream.
Footsteps weave a story rare,
Moving softly through the air.

With each beat, the silence breaks,
In rhythms that our passion makes.
A melody of soft embrace,
Together, lost in timeless space.

Fingers brush like silver light,
Guiding souls through the night.
Each twirl a spell, each glance a sigh,
In this dance, we learn to fly.

As the stars begin to fade,
In our hearts, the music played.
Together, we shall always roam,
In the dance that leads us home.

Colors of Tranquil Euphoria

In a field where wildflowers sway,
Colors blend at the break of day.
Petals whisper a secret tune,
Beneath the gaze of a gentle moon.

Soft blues blend with vibrant gold,
Stories of nature, quietly told.
Harmony finds its perfect place,
In the art of the universe's grace.

A canvas painted with dreams of light,
Where worries vanish out of sight.
Each hue a heartbeat, a silent prayer,
A tapestry woven with tender care.

In this moment, we find our peace,
As colors dance, our spirits release.
Tranquil euphoria fills the air,
A serene joy beyond compare.

Heartbeats in Harmony

Two souls linger in the night,
Heartbeats echo, soft and light.
In whispers shared, we find our tune,
A symphony beneath the moon.

With every pause, a breath we take,
Creating rhythms, love awake.
The world fades in this embrace,
In harmony, we find our place.

Like the waves that kiss the shore,
Ebbing gently, asking for more.
Each heartbeat matches the others' song,
Together, we know where we belong.

In this dance of give and receive,
We find the strength in what we believe.
Through night and day, we'll share this art,
Living life as heartbeats in harmony.

Lightness of Being

In the morning's tender glow,
A breeze whispers, soft and slow.
Each moment feels like a sigh,
Time floats gently, passing by.

Laughter dances on the air,
Gone are burdens, freed from care.
With each step, the spirit sings,
In the lightness that joy brings.

Clouds drift lazily above,
All around, the pulse of love.
In nature's arms, we lose our feet,
Finding solace, simple and sweet.

Every heartbeat, a feathered flight,
Embracing life, so pure and bright.
In this state of blissful grace,
We discover our sacred space.

Laughter of the Soul

In shadows cast and whispers heard,
A chuckle dances, light as a bird.
It weaves through silence, gentle and bright,
Laughter of the soul, a pure delight.

Each giggle echoes in the night sky,
Chasing away the tears that may lie.
With joy that springs from the heart so deep,
Laughter awakens dreams from their sleep.

In shared moments, bonds find their grace,
Smiles exchanged in a warm embrace.
Together we rise, together we fall,
In the laughter of the soul, we find it all.

Let the rhythm of joy, take its flight,
Guiding our spirits, igniting the light.
With every chuckle, our troubles unspooled,
In laughter, our hearts are lovingly schooled.

Hidden Gleams of Delight

In quiet corners, treasures reside,
Soft glimmers of joy that we often hide.
A smile that sparkles, a glance that ignites,
Hidden gleams of delight, in life's gentle lights.

In the rustle of leaves or the wink of a star,
Moments of magic that seem just afar.
They whisper to us, in the quiet of night,
Uncovering wonders bathed in pure light.

With a touch of kindness and a heart open wide,
We share these gleams, let the joy be our guide.
In laughter's embrace, we dance and we soar,
Finding delight in each moment and more.

For life is a canvas, painted with glee,
Hidden gems sparkle, for you and for me.
Let's cherish each jewel, let our hearts unite,
In these hidden gleams, we discover our light.

A Symphony of Inner Sunlight

Within the heart, a chorus sings,
Of sunlit whispers and golden wings.
Melodies flutter on gentle breeze,
A symphony of inner sunlight, it frees.

Every note carries warmth to the soul,
A dance of harmony, making us whole.
With vibrant hues, it colorizes the day,
In this radiant symphony, we find our way.

As dawn breaks open, threads of pure gold,
Stories of courage and love to be told.
Let the music swell, let the light ignite,
In the symphony of sunlight, all feels right.

Together we rise, a chorus anew,
Embracing the warmth, the love shining through.
With every heartbeat, let the singing start,
In this inner sunlight, we create art.

Glow of Serene Moments

In the stillness of dusk, a calm prevails,
Whispers of peace ride on soft, gentle gales.
With each breath taken, the world slows down,
Glow of serene moments, a soft, golden crown.

Gentle waves lapping on shores of the mind,
Echoing rhythms that soothe and unwind.
In these cherished pauses, where hope is unfurled,
We find gentle magic, a wondrous world.

Stars blink above in the evening's embrace,
Illuminating shadows, revealing their grace.
Holding onto silence, let our spirits roam,
In the glow of serene moments, we feel at home.

So let's linger long where the heart feels light,
In the embrace of stillness, everything feels right.
For in these small treasures, our souls understand,
The glow of serene moments, ever so grand.